Rollo the Viking: The Life and Legacy of the Viking Ruler Who Conquered Normandy

By Charles River Editors

A 12th century depiction of Vikings

About Charles River Editors

Charles River Editors is a boutique digital publishing company, specializing in bringing history back to life with educational and engaging books on a wide range of topics. Keep up to date with our new and free offerings with this 5 second sign up on our weekly mailing list, and visit Our Kindle Author Page to see other recently published Kindle titles.

We make these books for you and always want to know our readers' opinions, so we encourage you to leave reviews and look forward to publishing new and exciting titles each week.

Introduction

Michael Shea's picture of a statue of Rollo in Falaise

Rollo the Viking

"A cowardly man thinks he will ever live, if warfare he avoids; but old age will give no peace, though spears may spare him." – old Norse proverb from the Viking Age

In the autumn of 1911, an eye-watering mass of French citizens gathered around a churchyard in the heart of Rouen to celebrate the millennial anniversary of Normandy. A suspenseful hush fell over the congregation as a city official strode to the front of the crowd, placing his hands upon the large cloth draped over the mysterious statue. With a flick of his wrists, he unveiled an exquisite marble effigy of a handsome warrior, depicted with curly locks and a lush beard, with one hand wrapped around the handle of his sheathed sword as he gazed into the distance. The statue was of none other than Rollo the Viking, father of the Duchy of Normandy.

Over the centuries, the West has become fascinated by the Vikings, one of the most mysterious and interesting European civilizations. In addition to being perceived as a remarkably unique culture among its European counterparts, what's known and not known about the Vikings' accomplishments has added an intriguing aura to the historical narrative. Were they fierce and fearsome warriors? Were they the first Europeans to visit North America? It seems some of the legends are true, and some are just that, legend.

The commonly used term, Viking, for the trading and raiding peoples of Scandinavia may have originated from Viken (the large bay leading to Oslo), or it may have come from the Old Scandinavian words *Vikingr* (sea warrior) or *Viking* (expedition over the sea). The people from the north were known in Western Europe at the time as Northmen or Danes, in England as Danes or pagans and in Ireland as *Finngall* for those of Norwegian origin and *Dubgall* for those from Denmark. In the east, in Russia and in the Byzantine Empire, the Scandinavians were called *Vaeringar* or *Varyags* (Varangians) or *Rus'*, the latter perhaps derived from the name Roslagen, a province in Uppland in Sweden.

The ubiquitous picture of the Vikings as horn-helmeted, brutish, hairy giants that mercilessly marauded among the settlements of Northern Europe is based on a smattering of fact combined with an abundance of prejudicial historical writing by those who were on the receiving end of Viking depredations. At the same time, much of the popular picture of the Vikings is a result of the romantic imagination of novelists and artists. However, the Vikings' reputation for ferocious seaborne attacks along the coasts of Northern Europe is no exaggeration. It is true that the Norsemen, who traded extensively throughout Europe, often increased the profits obtained from their nautical ventures through plunder, acquiring precious metals and slaves. Of course, the Vikings were not the only ones participating in this kind of income generation; between the 8th and the 11th centuries, European tribes, clans, kingdoms and monastic communities were quite adept at fighting with each other for the purpose of obtaining booty. The Vikings were simply more successful than their contemporaries and thus became suitable symbols for the iniquity of the times. And among the Vikings, few were as successful as Rollo.

Rollo the Viking: The Life and Legacy of the Viking Ruler Who Conquered Normandy chronicles the life of the great warrior, dives into his many adventures and exploits, and examines just how this lone wolf managed to conquer his foes. Along with pictures depicting important people, places, and events, you will learn about Rollo the Viking like never before.

Rollo the Viking: The Life and Legacy of the Viking Ruler Who Conquered Normandy

About Charles River Editors

Introduction

   Remaking France

   Daring and Dangerous

   Unlikely Alliances

   The Land of the Franks

   Acquiring Normandy

   Online Resources

   Further Reading

Free Books by Charles River Editors

Discounted Books by Charles River Editors

Remaking France

"The summer moments always pass quickly." – Stanza 113 from the Hávamál (The Sayings of the High One), a 13th century poem from the Viking Age

The unraveling of the Western Roman Empire in the 5th century CE would clear the way for an unlikely, but ambitious force to not only enter, but conquer the region. These new contenders, who were at one point the very allies of the soon-to-be crippled empire, were the Franks. Having detected the frailty of the internally squabbling Romans, the Franks jumped on the opportunity to move into their territory, and they proceeded to do precisely that. In 451 CE, the Franks dispatched various vessels to the shores of the Roman-owned Germana Inferior, Belgica, and other areas of northern Gaul, and subjugated these villages. It was here that one of the grandest of all the Frankish monarchs, King Clovis, came to the fore.

Clovis was no older than 15 in 481 CE when he was awarded the royal scepter. Be that as it may, not only did the young king become the first monarch of what would become France, he proved to be a sharp-witted and competent ruler. In addition to triumphing in many battles, he also (some say strategically) converted and decreed the conversion of his Frankish subjects to Catholic Christianity. Whereas the Germanic peoples who usually plundered these parts were "Arian Christians" that discriminated against and oppressed their Roman Catholic slaves, Clovis's Catholicism aided in boosting his approval ratings with both existing subjects and the citizens of the new Roman lands he seized. Their ties to the Church also provided them with properly trained personnel sent from the institution, and the Christian missionaries were especially handy when it came to conciliating the conquered citizens. Furthermore, the Franks' retirement of the often corrupt and biased Roman taxation system, which largely contributed to the dissolution of the Western half of the empire, endeared the Franks to their subjects.

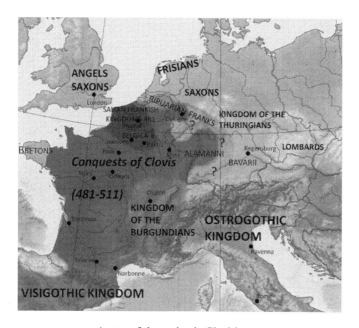

A map of the region in Clovis's era

The seeds planted by Clovis from his capital (now Paris) in Francia emboldened his successors to branch out at a pace unprecedented to their kind. By the start of the 7th century CE, Francia, the "Kingdom of the Franks," was possibly the most powerful of all the Germanic states that dominated the Western Romans. As it turned out, it was as difficult to achieve this distinction as it was to keep the land in their possession.

As per Germanic tradition, the properties of the Frankish kings were divvied up amongst their sons, giving way to multiple concurrent heirs and inevitable conflicts. First, they were halved into 3 kingdoms: Austrasia, which consisted of the original tribal territories (from what is now Belgium to northeast France); Neustria, comprising most of the Clovis-acquired lands in central France; and Burgundy. It was only in the late 600s that the Frankish kings, taking a page from the Romans, elected their own *major domus* ("mayors of the house"), known as *"major palatii."* They were to serve as the chief administrator of the Frankish palaces. In 687, Pepin II, or "Pepin of Herstal" *major palatii* of Austrasia, succeeded in regaining control of all 3 kingdoms for the first time in centuries. Following the death of Pepin II, his descendants scrambled for control until his illegitimate son, Charles Martel, emerged victorious. Martel, who spawned the Frankish Carolingian dynasty, was the grandfather of Holy Roman Emperor Charlemagne.

On top of the consolidation of Western Europe, Charlemagne fostered a renaissance that leapt over the Dark Ages and elevated the Carolingian empire's prosperity and prestige to new heights. For starters, his royal court was staffed only with academics and highly qualified officials, who supported him in his endeavors to enhance the local literature, art, and architectural scenes. He rescinded the gold standard and created a new currency system that revolved around the *livre*, a pound of silver, which streamlined and enriched their commerce. Most importantly, Charlemagne, a "sponsor of medieval education," established a string of schools and did plenty to refine the curriculum, which resulted in skyrocketing literacy rates.

Unfortunately, the Frankish custom of equal inheritance soon robbed the gold from this gilded era. Upon the demise of Louis the Pious, son of Charlemagne, Francia was split once more between Charlemagne's grandsons via the 843 Treaty of Verdun. West Francia, made up of what is mostly modern-day France, was allotted to Charles the Bald. "Middle Kingdom," made up of a narrow strip of territories from Frisia to Italy, as well as bits of modern Switzerland and Germany, was bestowed upon Lothar I. Finally, Louis the German was given East Francia, which included territories in Germany, Poland, and other areas that ultimately became the Holy Roman Empire.

Among the people zeroing in on the problematic, but prosperous Francia were the Vikings. The rich resources and the abundance of tillable land in the Frankish kingdom were all well and good, but it was the wealth of noble homes and poorly guarded churches and monasteries, all presumably overflowing with treasure, that lured them to the foreign land. Much to the Vikings' disappointment, they were thwarted by the well-defended river systems under Charlemagne's reign, but as the Franks had done to the Western Romans, the Vikings patiently lurked in the shadows, waiting for the perfect chance to pounce.

Though the coastal communities of Francia had been pestered by sporadic ambushes from the Vikings for decades, Frankish rulers were much too preoccupied with their tug-of-war over authority to wise up to this impending threat. Unbeknownst to them, not only were their river defenses slipping, the Vikings had now infiltrated the British Isles, and they had even flown their flag in Ireland. In fact, an assault was soon to befall them, one that would spark a century-long series of incursions in France that ultimately dismantled the once invincible Carolingian empire.

On the 24th of June, 843 CE, the joyous inhabitants of the city of Nantes, which lies by the River Loire in southern Brittany, poured into the streets to commemorate the *Fête de la Saint-Jean*, or the "Festival of Saint John." The fair organized for this occasion bustled with song and chatter, mostly from merchants peddling candles, effigies, and other religious tokens to pilgrims as they headed for the city cathedral. As the entire city was invited to the fair, Mass, and midsummer bonfire, authorities had carelessly left their entrances unlocked and unmanned.

With all of Nantes gathered in the city square, a band of hooded gentlemen who had quietly disembarked from 67 ships crept past the creaking city gates. Upon finding the fair, they immediately blended in with the other hooded guests, most of them merchants from faraway villages. But these cloaked men, who soundlessly interspersed themselves among the crowd, were not interested in the textiles or metal products the local smithies had to offer. Rather, they were veiled Vikings stalking their prey, who would not remain blissfully unaware much longer. Once they became convinced that their victims were at their most vulnerable, the Vikings cast off their hoods and drew the weapons concealed in their cloaks.

Armed with axes and swords, the Vikings hacked their way to the front of the congregation, slaying citizens, monks, and clergymen left and right. Bishop Saint Gohard (or Gohardus) of Nantes tried to repel these rogues as best he could, but he, too, would fall victim to the Vikings' blades. It was pure pandemonium as stampedes of panicking citizens trampled over the bodies strewn across the space and attempted to barricade themselves in the Churches of Saint Paul and Saint Peter, but the invaders burst through the flimsy doors and disemboweled every last one in sight. An eyewitness account graphically described the bloodbath: "Children hanging on their dead mothers' breasts drank blood rather than milk...the stone flags of the church ran red with the blood of holy men and the holy altar dripped the blood of innocents...The pagans then pillaged all the city, seized all its treasures, and set fire to the [churches]. They then took a great number of prisoners as hostages for ransom, and returned to their ships..."

The ravaging did not cease here. The Vikings sailed up the Loire and sacked the monasteries in Vertou, Indres, and northern Poitou, and they subsequently harassed the coastal cities of Aquitaine before taking a breather in Noirmoutier for the winter. The following year, the same Viking ships glided along the rough waters of the River Garonne in southwest France, plundering, pillaging, and torching the towns and villages along the way, going as far as Toulouse.

It was at this point that the major powers of Europe began to view the Vikings as a serious threat for the first time. Before 843, the Vikings had never attempted so subdue such a major settlement within the Carolingian Empire, but while the death and destruction brought about these pillagers – unnamed Vikings from Vestfold – certainly left an indelible impression upon the survivors and their neighboring towns, many say their wrath was nothing compared to a vicious and vindictive Viking by the name of "Rollo," who would soon make his debut.

Daring and Dangerous

Like most other figures in early history, Rollo's roots, muddled by contradicting accounts, are shrouded in mystery. Medieval chroniclers from Norway and Iceland assert that Rollo and Gange-Rolv (otherwise known as Rolv Ganger), the Viking chieftain most famed for his adventures in France, were one and the same. Modern Danish historians, on the other hand, scoff at these claims, and insist that Rollo was Danish. In spring of 2014, a report published by one

Michael R. Maglio announced that the DNA extracted from the remnants of Rollo's descendants disclosed them to be of Danish origin, but this theory was discredited a few years later when a separate team revealed that the original researchers had misidentified the examined corpses. Thus, while there exists no concrete evidence that supports either one of these claims, the majority of European experts today agree with the former.

It was the French monk and historian Richerus of Reims who first made a reference to Rollo's roots in the late 10th century (between 996 and 998). Rollo, affirmed Richerus, was the son of Catillus, or Ketil, who may have been one of the thousands of Vikings that massacred the festival-goers in Nantes. Such a possibility was considered until recently, when historians concluded Catillus was a fictitious character of lore.

A historian of early Norman history, Dudo of St. Quentin, surfaced a century later, and he painted an entirely different account. Rollo, he claimed, along with his brother, Gurim, or "Gorm," were sons of an influential noble in Dacia, described by Dudo as a territory that generally corresponds to modern-day Denmark. Dudo's version of events was partially echoed by the 12th century *Orkneyinga Saga*, along with the *Landnámabók*, the *Hemskringla*, and a slew of other Icelandic sources. In these recollections, Rollo is identified as "Hrólfr," son of the earl of Møre, but rather than Dacia, it was in Iceland that they settled. Moreover, Rollo's brother, Gorm, is not mentioned in any of these accounts.

Owing to the inconsistent and convoluted state of the information in current circulation, it only makes sense to pluck the most widely repeated elements from various accounts in order to piece together a coherent timeline of Rollo's fascinating life and conquests.

Rollo was born around the year 846 to the founding Earl Roegnwald (or Rognvald Eysteinsson) of Møre and his wife, Hilldur. Besides maintaining his domain in Dacia – which, though labeled as "Denmark" by Dudo, encompassed lands in Moldova, Romania, Hungary, Bulgaria, and Ukraine – Roegnwald, who bred a legion of fierce warriors, went on to dominate numerous more cities, and hegemonized the people there. Needless to say, Roegnwald had an exalted status and fearsome reputation; in Dudo's words, he was a "man who never lowered the nape of his neck before any king, nor placed his hands in anyone else's hands in committing himself to service." As such, Rollo was left with some enormous boots to fill.

There is little known about Rollo's childhood, but historians assume that he received an upbringing similar to that of a typical Viking. As dictated by the ancient Norse custom, the decision to rear Rollo, like all Viking children, was contingent on his physical condition and potential for strength. While not all Viking parents discarded children born with birth defects, many were known to abandon their "flawed" young ones. Bearing this in mind, Roegnwald, often depicted as a brawny and pragmatic Viking traditionalist, would have most likely deserted Rollo had he been anything other than a healthy baby boy. Additionally, approximately 17% of children at the time failed to see puberty. Considering these statistics, it would be fair to surmise that Rollo had been blessed with an exceptional immune system.

Once Viking kids were weaned, they were left on their lonesome or in the company of their siblings. Since Hilldur had her hands full with the management of the household and the family farm, and Roegnwald had a daily circuit around his dependencies, even as a child, Rollo was predominantly left to his own devices. To entertain himself, he probably pranced around with his legs clamped around sticks, and fenced his siblings and other neighbor children with planks of roughly cut wood, perhaps recreating scenes of his father's tussles in his own backyard. Spotting the promising agility and natural fighting ability in his son, Roegnwald encouraged him to keep up with the "play-acting," for sharpening his reflexes at an early age could only help with his future prowess on the battlefield.

Roegnwald, like most Vikings, was more concerned with the development of practical skills than they he was with formal education. That being said, a few Viking boys, particularly those from wealthier families, were taught how to read and write the Dacian runic alphabet, for rudimentary literacy still bore weight in Viking circles. Whether or not Rollo was provided with such a privilege is unverified, but taking his aristocratic status into account, to say that he was granted at least some basic education in this field would be a reasonable presumption. Nonetheless, Rollo learned the majority of his life lessons from the tales told to him by his father and elders.

Rollo was not given a shiny toy, nor was he presented with his favorite meal for his 10th birthday. Instead, he was accorded a gift deemed far more honorable in the eyes of the Vikings: responsibility. He was made to pitch in on the family farm, planting crops, tending livestock, and performing arduous manual labor normally reserved for adults twice his size. He might have also been personally trained by Roegnwald, or sent to a male relative for some time, in the art of trading.

Apart from the virtues of independence and self-sustenance, Roegnwald hoped to reinforce Rollo's self-defense skills. Thus, the 10-year-old graduated from sparring to small-scale, but legitimate single combats, primarily arranged by the adults in the community. Viking children who faced off no longer wielded wooden weapons, but actual spears, swords, and axes, some forged in the then-revolutionary material of crucible steel. Archaeologist and Assistant Professor at the Institute of Archaeology of Rzeszów University in Poland Lezek Gardela explained, "The games were very physical and often brutal, sometimes even ending in serious wounds or deaths of the participants."

These Viking games were designed to test the "strength, dexterity, and cunning" of the younglings. One example was the Viking variation of wrestling. The physically weakest were the first to be thrust into the ring, and the winner of the match then squared off with the next competitor until there remained only one standing. Stone lifting tournaments were another way to put their muscles to the test. Ball games – such as *knattleikr*, a sport that some liken to a hybrid of modern hockey and cricket – that involved heavy, full-body contact were also played by Rollo regularly to heighten his swiftness, attentiveness, and obstacle evasion. These games, especially for the aggressively competitive and fiery-tempered Rollo, likely ended quite frequently with fractured *knattleikr* bats and broken noses.

Most Vikings married by the age of 20, with some Viking girls married off as young as age 12, but the dashing Rollo went against this tradition. While Rollo, who had grown from an adorable, blue-eyed blond kid into a broad-shouldered, strikingly handsome young man with a thick flaxen mane, certainly had plenty of maidens, he could not be tied down, for in his heart lay only one true love: adventure.

Rollo quickly became the object of affection of the Dacian young women and the envy of all men. Apart from his apparently knee-weakening good looks – the gaze of his "fiercely blue eyes" so potent that it could "command the roughest sea robber and bring him to his will" – he was well-built and extraordinarily tall. He was so tall, in fact, that there was not a single horse that could carry a man of his imposing stature. This was what earned him the sobriquet "Rollo" or "Rolv the Walker." Others say it was because his feet dragged across the ground whenever he rode one of these unfortunate stallions.

It was not merely Rollo's height, his attractiveness, or the glinting golden arm bands and amulets stamped with the hammer of Thor he sported that made him such a captivating character. His storytellers say he was as effortlessly charismatic as he was intimidating. With one raise of his right hand, those around him instantly fell silent, yet at the same time, said Dudo, his "mouth flowed with honey."

When it became clear that the restless and "wild-blooded" Rollo was no longer content in Dacia, Roegnwald constructed for him a fleet of 6 warships. Each was decked out with shields along the sides, about half to a dozen oars fashioned out of pine, and its own crew, many of them veteran Vikings, or *thegn*, who had sailed the high seas and confronted foes alongside Roegnwald himself. As Roegnwald was endowed with more than enough funds to do so, these war vessels, known alternatively as "dragons" or *"longships,"* would have been state-of-the-art models that could withstand tempestuous tides and stormy weathers, as well as cruise across shallow waters, thanks to its draft (the distance between the waterline and the hull) of 20 inches. The prows and sterns of these skinny, durable longships were often ornamented with the heads of dragons, serpents, and other mighty and symbolic beasts. In Rollo's case, his most likely featured the head of a lion.

A Viking ship

In his early 20s, or maybe even younger, Rollo, who had always aspired to become a "sea rover," was finally given free rein to pursue his ambitions. To live a life of a sea rover was to be a swashbuckling pirate on both sea and land, feeding on chaos and the treasures of their victims, but this was considered a respectable profession during the Viking Age. Even those who earned their bread and butter by farming and trade took occasional hiatuses to partake in these expeditions.

It was King Harald Fairhair (sometimes credited as Prettyhair), the first royal sovereign of Norway, who presided over Dacia at the time. Harald, hailed by medieval chroniclers as "one of the greatest 9th century Scandinavian warrior chiefs," was a belligerent, but competent ruler. Though his jurisdiction was technically only confined to the western coastal villages, he indirectly controlled other Norwegian communities through trusty chieftains stationed in each of these localities. This meant that a hefty portion, if not all of the tolls and tariffs collected from these distant villages landed in Harald's treasury.

Earls like Roegnwald were also appointed by Harald and charged with preserving and dispensing justice, as well as tax collection. They were granted a percentage of the collected duties, but they were expected to augment the royal troops if the situation called for it. While this system did much to stabilize and improve Norway's annual economic income, only those in the upper echelons lavished in the kingdom's riches. On the other end of the spectrum, small-time landowners, farmers, merchants, and Vikings in lower classes were left disenfranchised. The most disgruntled were those who were forcibly evicted from their homes for their failure to cough up the stifling taxes.

The displaced Danishes, Norwegians, and other Nordic folk who previously resided in Harald's territories sought their fortunes across the North Sea, and many wound up in Scotland, the Faroe Islands, the Orkneys, Finland, and other areas that dotted the southern coast of the Baltic. Some cut their losses and shook off their grudges (a few even participated in trade with Norway and Harald's domains later on), but others harbored unwavering animosity towards the king. Much to the king's umbrage, one of these vagabond scoundrels was the son of his own *consigliere*, the Earl of Møre, and he would soon prove to be much more than a pest.

Harald took no issue with the Vikings ransacking the villages of foreign lands, the key word here being "foreign." There was only one rule the Vikings were to abide by, which was to steer clear of the kingdom's or its sister territories, and it was this golden rule that Rollo chose to break. What made this all the more perplexing and infuriating to Harald was that Rollo was neither strapped for cash, tax-wise or otherwise, nor was he in danger of being ejected from his land. As such, the king chalked his disobedience up to greed and regarded it as a personal attack.

At first, Harald turned a grudging blind eye to Rollo's transgressions, for the young voyager, who harried the villages by the restricted East Sea, was insulated by his father's connections. The last straw, however, came one summer in the mid-870s when Rollo, upon returning from another raid, decided to make a stop in Viken, a district in southeastern Norway). There, Rollo and his men slaughtered dozens of farmers, cattle-handlers, and their families before making off with several herds of cattle.

An enraged Harald organized a conference with his lawmakers and lawspeakers, known as an Alþing, or a "Thing," at once. In their presence, Harald branded Rollo a national criminal and ordered for him to be expelled from Dacia, effective immediately. Roegnwald and Hilldur lamented the charge and beseeched the king's forgiveness on behalf of their delinquent son, but there was no changing Harald's mind. Hilldur wailed, "You then expel my dearest son (named after my father)! The lion whom you exile, is the bold progeny of a noble race. Why, O King, are you thus violent?"

With no choice but to comply with Harald's decree of eternal banishment, Rollo and his men boarded their 6 ships and sailed off towards the setting winter sun. Though he maintained his composure, the Viking captain, or *skeppare*, was devastated at having been blacklisted. While those around him delighted at the thought of the thrilling escapades and boundless treasure awaiting them in this never-ending adventure, celebrating with music, miming performances, mummeries, and boisterous drinking games, the disoriented Rollo, who previously thought himself untouchable, consumed goblet after goblet of ale and mead in solitude. The merry crewmen jigged and toasted to the "tyranny" they were leaving behind, but for the first time in his life, the once-raging flame of confidence and determination inside the now aimless Rollo began to flicker.

This flame would not be reignited until several days after Rollo and his men docked their ships along the shores of Scanza (or Scania, now Sweden). Following some self-reflection, Rollo, who was more livid than he was disconsolate, decided that it was now his chief objective not only to return to Dacia, but to dethrone Harald and claim the land for himself. He then continued to wrestle with this until one evening, when the tossing and turning Rollo slipped into an "anxious" slumber and was visited by none other than Odin himself. The soothing and silvery *vox divina* (divine voice) of the almighty Norse god called out to Rollo as he wandered through the dreamscape: "Arise swiftly. Hurry across the ocean's deep waters, straightaway to the Angles."

The following morning, Rollo traveled into town and consulted the local sages about his cryptic dream. Only one thought himself able to read between the lines of the literal context, saying unto him, "At a future time, you will come to the Angles...where you will become a savior...[and where] you will have the glory of everlasting peace, free from harm...And in the course of time, you will be purified by baptism, and will become a worthy Christian...[by the power] of the *angeli* (angels)."

Rollo was puzzled, and frankly he was unimpressed by the final part of the sage's prediction, but nevertheless, the *skeppare* rounded up his men and headed for "Angles," or Anglia, the predecessor of England. Catching sight of the approaching Viking longships on the horizon, the best and boldest Anglian warriors grabbed hold of their swords and bows and lined themselves along the shore, ready to defend themselves, but try as they might, they would be no match for Rollo and his seasoned warriors. The giant of a man slashed open the chests of thousands of villagers with all the force of a beast freshly released from its cage and all the nonchalance of a jogger out on his afternoon run, his gilded helmet and mail armor gleaming under the scorching midday sun. When the locals finally surrendered, Rollo's men stripped the valuables off the dead's bodies and buried their corpses. Shackled captives, many of them local leaders and politicians, were marched onto the Vikings' ships, where they would be assorted, tagged, and later sold off to slave traders.

As Rollo scanned his surroundings, studying the blood and carnage by his feet, the whimpers of the hostages muffled through the ships behind him, he was more clueless than ever. Had he acted too rashly by taking the advice of a strange, disembodied voice from his dream? If not, where was he to go from here? Should he go back to Dacia? Or was he to remain in and take Anglia for himself, where he was promised "everlasting peace" and bottomless riches?

Unlikely Alliances

"A wary guest who to reflection comes, keeps a cautious silence; with his ears listens, and with his eyes observes: so explores every prudent man." – An ancient proverb from the Viking Age

While the bound hostages awaited their dreadful fates, deprived of food, water, and personal space, Rollo attempted to make up his addled mind. The rest of the survivors had already pledged their loyalties to the invader and his henchmen, but still, Rollo was uncertain about his next step. Opting to forgo what he feared were premature celebrations, he retired to the temporary camp the Vikings had erected and willed himself to some much-needed sleep. He allowed himself to succumb to the swirling stars and twinkling spasms of color behind his sealed eyelids, and soon teleported to a snow-crested mountaintop in Francia. Trickling down the peak was a fragrant and winding stream with rustling waters as clear as glass. Instinctively, Rollo, who felt himself "polluted by leprosy and lust," peeled off his clothes and cleansed himself in the comfortable warm water.

When Rollo stepped out of the spring to dry off, a brilliant flurry consisting of thousands of birds appeared above him, a bevy so massive it seemed to cover every inch of azure in the sky. Squinting northward, Rollo noted that the birds, which came in every color imaginable, shared identical scarlet left wings. And there, Rollo stood, gawking at the wondrous sight, until, without warning, the single-minded mass of birds swooped down towards him. Much to Rollo's relief, the birds flew past him, enveloping him only in a strong gust of wind from their flapping wings as they perched upon the mountain stream. Once they had bathed themselves, some birds began to peck at the verdant pasture, while others gathered twigs, leaves, and earth for their nests. Finally, the birds came as one upon the grass, looking up at Rollo, towering above them, with their shiny, beady eyes, as if submitting to him "willingly as an empire."

As soon as his eyes fluttered open the next morning, Rollo summoned the *thegn* and the collection of sages he had captured from his previous expeditions, and demanded that they interpret the second prophecy. Stumped, all of them remained silent, staring sheepishly at their shuffling feet, all but the sage who had advised him to come to Angles to fulfill his Christian destiny. "The mountain of Francia that you seemed to stand on, suggests what rises there [and also symbolizes the Church of France]. The fountain at the summit of the mountain is explained as one of rebirth [and also represents holy baptism]. You shall understand how horrible and base the deeds you do truly are, for you were corrupted by most of them. Now, you were washed in that fountain and purged; you were born again and lost your sins." The birds (or as stated by other sources, bees), the wiseman continued, signified men from different provinces, and their red wings, a metaphor for the shields they toted. These men, he claimed, were Rollo's future subjects, or his *fideles*. Like Rollo, his subjects were awash with sin, hence the birds' dip in the spring. To rectify this, they were to undergo baptism and be cleansed through "communal living." Last, but not least, the building of the nests was God's way of instructing Rollo to rebuild the towns he razed to the ground.

Rollo's reservations about the Christian elements in his visions remained largely unabated, but he was so impressed by the exhaustive interpretation that he unshackled the sage at once and sent him off to live his life as a free man. After mulling it over, he elected to play by the rules of the mysterious dream-weaver, and in the following days, he freed every last ones of the hostages on his longships. His men were bewildered by such a request, but few voiced their opinions, and the allegiant cronies did as they were told. Lo and behold, the unshackled were so grateful for their freedom that they showered their captors with gifts, including hacksilver and silver ingots, which the Vikings used as a currency.

As maintained by Dudo, it was at this stage that Rollo forged an unexpected friendship with the local ruler, King Alstem. The identity of this nonexistent "King Alstem" also continues to be a matter of dispute. Some theorize that it was Alfred the Great, King of Wessex, that Dudo was referring to, but most historians – despite the conflicting timeline – believe he was Guthrum, the Danish king of East Angles whom Alfred the Great baptized and christened "Athelstan."

A few days later, a group of envoys sent by Rollo appeared before King Alstem and delivered to him the following message: "Our patrician Rollo, the most distinguished duke of the Dacians, sends faithful service to you, and the gift of unshattered [sic] friendship to your followers. Through great misfortune in Dacia, he was fraudulently banished. The wind blew us this way...Sir, we will not pillage your realm, nor in any way bring plundered booty to our ships. We seek a negotiated peace so that we can buy and sell for a while. And when spring comes, we shall depart for Francia."

Alstem, who had learned of the Vikings' mischief and their dramatic change of heart, including the ongoing reconstruction of the Anglian town, was appalled by the needless deaths, but he was also moved by their display of remorse. Taking a leap of faith and exhibiting the grace he was renowned for, or perhaps smelling a mutually beneficial partnership in the making, Alstem set his grievances aside, and asked to meet with Rollo in person. Wasting no time, Rollo entered the royal chambers, and following a pleasant discussion and a cordial and contractual embrace, the enterprising pair came to an agreement.

Alstem outlined the terms of their pact in the following declaration: "Let us be joined in a single favorable alliance of faith. Be always, I beg, a part of my soul and my companion...And I earnestly beseech you to remain in our territory...Come, keep whatever you desire in the orbit of our authority. [But] always be mindful of me in everything, just as I myself shall be [to you]...And if at some time this savage, untameable...impudent nation...should fight against me, bring such assistance as you are able, saving me with a steadfast effort. And I will assist you, helping in a similar fashion...My shield will cover you in our common struggle."

However, Rollo made it clear that he had no intention of extending his stay in Angles: "Thank you, great king, for these willing boons. I will not stay very long in your realm, but go to Francia as swiftly as I am able. There I will remain your friend till the end, united in an alliance of indissoluble esteem."

In the months leading up to the summertime, Rollo and his men patched up and added to their fleet of longships, a process that was accelerated by the assisting villagers. Many of them – mostly reformed criminals, unemployed mercenaries, ill-starred merchants, and other misfits of society – joined and received training from the Viking generals, increasing the size of Rollo's crew.

When stripes of white and purple began to streak across the Anglian lilies, the telltale signs of summer's bloom, Rollo and his men piled into their ships and sailed southward, bound for Francia. For the first few days, the longships floated across the tranquil waters, ushered forth by the gentle summer breeze. Then, out of nowhere, the longships were pummeled by a freak storm that veered them off course, possibly another omen of sorts. Those that weren't tossed out by the violently rocking ships clung on to the railings for their dear lives as the gray sky flashed and cackled above them. They could hear the unmistakable cracks of their splintering oars, broken by the howling winds. Buckets of water splashed onto the swaying ships, soaking the Vikings and loosening their weakening grips. Legend has it that Rollo crawled to the center of his longship to add some balance to the unsteady vessel, and laid flat on his back. He then stretched out his arms and squeezed his eyes shut, roaring at the swirling skies: "You, who, through the gift of a vision, wish troublesome me, filled with the vices of sin and with impurity – restrain these fierce billows of a violent whirlpool, and hold back, and calm the deep!"

In that instant, the storm abruptly ceased. Likewise, the turbulent waves suddenly became still, and the leaden clouds above them parted, as if the bizarre storm had never even transpired. Most have written off this event, if genuine, as nothing more than a coincidence, but some, such as the crewmen who supposedly witnessed this miracle, became persuaded of Rollo's supernatural powers, vested in him by the Great Odin. Dudo, on the other hand, claimed that Rollo had directed his plea to the "Omnipotent God" of the Christians, and that it was the granting of his prayers that pushed him to take the first step upon the path towards the Lord.

It appeared to Rollo that this freak storm was no accident at all, for between the curtains of the clearing fog and mist was the glowing coast of the Walgri (the shores of Western Netherlands). Like those in Angles, the Walgrians who had seen the incoming ships, accompanied by villagers who lived by the River Waal, scrambled for their swords, determined to fend off the intruders. Pumped with adrenaline and newly empowered by the inexplicable miracle at sea, Rollo trudged out from his ship and tore open the Walgrians with his swinging sword. His resilient men pulled themselves together at once and followed suit, knocking down the defenders of the land with their axes, almost as if they hadn't just been on the brink of death.

Firmly believing that his destiny now lay in Walgri, Rollo ordered his men to lay siege to the Waal region. Since they were by now consummate marauders and subjugators, it did not take long for the Vikings to batter and bedevil the locals into submission. About a week or so later, Alstem, who had caught wind of the Vikings' detour to Walgri, dutifully shipped over a dozen boats packed to the ceilings with barrels of grain, wine, and lard, amongst other supplies, as well as another dozen containing readily-armed soldiers. Thoroughly pleased by the consignments, Rollo sent a few representatives back to Angles bearing treasures from Walgri as a gesture of gratitude and goodwill.

Alstem, now in the midst of a great rebellion, was in dire need of assistance. Now that he had held up his end of the bargain, he expected Rollo to reciprocate. He attached the following message to Rollo's envoys and sent them back to Walgri: "This realm, which I rule and profit, is being laid waste, and the dignity of my rule being brought to nothing, for the Angles, elated and corrupted by rash haughtiness, are unwilling to obey my commands. Falling away from me, they have conspired among themselves, and rejecting me and my service...even snatch for themselves the profits of my small towns [his territories in what is now the Netherlands, Denmark, and maybe Belgium]. Thus I pray you to help me dash them to pieces and scatter them and crush them and tread down their insolent strength, so that they be brought back, even if unwilling, to my service, and sharply undergo whatever punishment they deserve."

For this, Alstem continued, he pledged to give Rollo not just the "moiety of [his] own goods," but "half the store of all [his] household furnishings" and "half of his realm." Rollo was thrilled by the generous offer, but did not seem too interested in ruling half of Angles, for he desired nothing more than to fulfill the prophecy in Francia. Even so, being a man of his word, he resolved to honor the pact, and vowed to bring the anarchists and renegades to justice.

In retrospect, the Walgrians might have been spared the butchery that would soon befall them had they capitulated to the Vikings, but the Walgrians refused to tolerate anyone who dared to steal their motherland. Initially, local authorities were under the impression that this was no different than any other "hit-and-run" Viking raid, and as such, they ordered what was left of their outnumbered defenders to stand down until the enemies became satiated by their plunders, which normally took no more than a day. But when the Vikings continued to rifle through their granaries, one day after another, signaling their plans to stay indefinitely, the Walgrians called upon a couple men from allied districts for assistance: Ragnar Longneck (AKA Reginar I Longneck), Count of Hainaut, and Frisian Prince Radbod. The identity of Radbod is yet another matter that has yet to be resolved, for there is no room for the real Radbod, who ruled a century earlier, in this timeline. Most assume that storytellers meant either Count Rorik or Gerulf I of Frisia.

In spite of his crude exterior, Rollo was highly astute and possessed an intuition like no other. Having anticipated the arrival of Longneck and Radbod's armies long before their actual appearance, the Vikings secreted themselves behind a dense cluster of trees and waited for the soldiers to saunter right into their trap. Sure enough, as soon as the reinforcements arrived, the Vikings sprang forth and launched themselves on their enemies, thousands falling under their swords.

The skirmish showcased the Vikings' aptitude for adapting to just about any battle situation. No longer facing a disorderly rabble of civilians-turned-defenders, but a mass of royally trained soldiers, the Vikings formed a wedge formation (otherwise known as the "Flying V") with their finest fighters, called *"berserkers,"* fronting the inverted pyramid. Those in the middle and rear of the formation hurled javelins as they charged towards their opponents.

Although Rollo had predicted their arrival, he was greatly angered by the ambush, and even more frustrated by what felt like the endless obstacles to his prophecy, if such a thing even existed. Rollo commanded his men to set the town ablaze, and once they had gathered suspected insurgents against Alstem, along with several slaves for good measure, and shipped them off to Angles, his men annihilated what was left of the civilians. He then dusted off his hands and ordered his men to move into the neighboring strongholds to exact his revenge on Longneck and Radbod.

The Vikings arrived first in Zuiderzee, the territory of the latter, and when they had vacuumed up the valuables from the entire town, they proceeded to squash the locals who vainly attempted to stand their ground. The Frisians had not only underestimated the size of Rollo's force, like the Walgrians, they had vastly undervalued their mastery of the battlefield. Frisian soldiers barreled towards them in droves, only to hit an unbreakable wall of oblong shields, otherwise referred to as a *"skjaldborg."* The Vikings also positioned themselves in a variation of the Flying V known as the *svinfylking*, or "boar formation," essentially "triangular wedges" of 20-30 warriors, "tapered back on each side from the center point to make a tight spearhead." Emulating the charge of a boar, they rammed the shield walls of their opponents with the "spearhead." When the Frisians became sufficiently dazed, the *svinfylking* dismantled, allowing the warriors fastest on their feet to either capture or behead the generals. These generals, along with more insurgents, slaves, and a shipload of Zuiderzee treasures, were then transported back to Angles.

With one of the Frisians' major cities now reduced to burnt rubble, Rollo and his men boarded their ships and sailed towards the Scheldt, a 220-mile-long river that slithers down southwestern Netherlands, western Belgium, and northern France, where they call it the *"l'Escaut."* The Vikings stopped their ships just before drifting into Belgian territory and unloaded themselves on the shore where Longneck's stronghold resided.

For the first time since Rollo's departure from Angles, the Vikings, now drained and spent from the continual warfare, encountered some trouble with the resistance. The morning Rollo and his men tackled the Hainautians by the local abbey, they only just managed to capture Longneck after barely suppressing his men. That same afternoon, the fatigued Vikings were assailed by another band of Hainautian soldiers from the rear, and after letting their guards slip, allowed at least 12 of the *thegn* to be taken prisoner.

Desperate for the safe return of her husband, Longneck's wife, Hersinda, orchestrated a hostage exchange with the Vikings through her officials. But Rollo, humiliated by the defeat, refused to play ball. The Hainautian officials were tasked with bringing this message back to her: "Unless you first hand over my companions to me, Ragnar will not be returned to you, but will lose his head. And what is more, give me all the gold and silver there is in his [county] – the whole tribute payment of that region." With her better half's life at stake, Hersinda and her officials filled multiple sacks with all the gold and silver available to them, as well as the costly offerings displayed at the sacred altars and the precious metals they prised off their churches, and delivered them to Rollo, along with the *thegn*. The Vikings rejoiced at the glittering mounds of treasure presented to them, but Rollo, who had been given some time to ruminate on the savage and purposeless destruction he was causing, again had another change of heart. He sent for Longneck and proposed to him a peaceful resolution to their problems in the form of an ultimatum: "Duke Ragnar, what wrong had I ever done you when you went to battle along with the Walgri and Frisians against me? If you now desire to vent your rage, the arrows and armed retainers of war are wanting. If you wish to slip away in fright, you cannot escape while entangled in fetters..."

When he became convinced that Longneck would uphold the ceasefire, he continued, "As I did with the Frisians, I have retaliated for the evils you brought on me without cause. In exchange for you, your wife and your leaders have sent me all the gold and silver they were able to find. I will hand over to you half of the gathered tribute and send you back to your wife. Rest after this while growing mild. Let there in no way be discord between me and you, but rather everlasting, peaceful friendship." And with that, another adventitious friendship was forged.

Rollo and his men continued to camp out in the Netherlands until about 876 (others contend that it was in the early 880s), coexisting harmoniously with the locals as they, once again, reassembled what they had destroyed. He might have very well settled down here for the rest of his days had it not been for the third vision he received late one evening. "Rollo," said the familiar voice, penetrating the onyx-black around him. "Tarrying in the Netherlands...you took more than enough revenge on all your foes. When time is ready, you will suffer the battles and be greatly harassed by the Aquitanian Wars. After this, baptized, you will capture rewards. Among them is the present of never-ending life."

In light of this revelation, Rollo and his men bade farewell to their new allies, and set sail to the northwestern region of Francia, or as it is known today, Normandy.

The Land of the Franks

"Fortune has harassed you with many complaints,

Whence you have endured many kinds of threats and very great hardships.

Forthwith will it thenceforth offer you better things, with everlasting success,

Joyous things will now follow so many rough ones, tolerated for so long..." – Excerpt of a prophecy for Rollo, according to Dudo of St. Quentin

The now dizzying fleet of longships came across Jumieges by the River Seine, but rather than throw down their anchors, they sailed towards the opposite side of the mainland and moored their ships to the pierside of a now-demolished St. Vedast Chapel. At long last, after 3 visions, Rollo, along with the better part of the Vikings, no longer had any doubts that their fates lay in the hands of the Christian God. To somewhat formalize his newfound piousness to the deity, he uncased several intricately carved effigies of the Virgin Saint Hameltrude in stone and bronze and placed them upon the chapel altar. These statues, which were gifted to him before he left Angles, were tokens of the Anglian Church's appreciation. His unveiling of these statues, which had been stowed away in one of his ships for months (or years) collecting dust, demonstrates that he was now ready to fight in the name of the Lord. St. Vedast was later renamed "St. Hameltrude" by the residents.

A few mornings later, those who lived in the nearby village of Rouen (now the capital of Normandy) awoke to the sobering news of the Vikings' presence in Jumieges. Since the village was populated by mainly impoverished farmers and beaten merchants who were scraping by on a good day, they knew that there was no way they could stave off the Vikings. Village leaders made a beeline for the office of Bishop Franco of Rouen and implored him to reach out to the intruders. Having heard of the spate of horror stories suffered by the defenseless inhabitants in Viking-besieged villages, Bishop Franco sent an envoy to Jumieges to negotiate an understanding between them post-haste.

The soft-spoken messenger sent by Franco tentatively welcomed the foreigners to their land. He then beckoned Rollo towards the river bank and invited him to gaze upon the dilapidated wasteland that was Rouen across the Seine. While the treasure they could afford to part with did not amount to even half of the Vikings' usual bounties, the Rouenians were willing to share their territories, resources, and portion of their profits with the Vikings. In return, they humbly requested the Vikings' protection, as well as a "guarantee of safety" for all those who dwelled in the district.

Apparently, Rollo felt what can only be described as pity for the defenseless Rouenians, and, moved by their initiative, he agreed to the pact. The Vikings headed back on the Seine and tethered their longships to the gate of Rouen's St. Martin Church. There, they solicited and received newly-minted armors, weapons, and battle supplies, as well as vessels of whatever food the people could spare. The transaction, as Rollo had assured them it would be, was a peaceful one.

Just as there were a few Vikings who were more than resistant to abandoning their pagan faith, there were Christian locals who questioned Franco's allegiance with Rollo, one that many claimed was akin to making a pact with the devil. Some went so far as to petition the pope to show his hand, protesting to him in a letter, "With heathens…[even] when they have been baptized and rebaptized…[they] carry on living as Heathens, killing Christians as the Heathens do, slaughtering priests, and eating animals that have been sacrificed to their idols." To their dismay, their concerns were cast aside. The pope urged them to remain patient with the unorthodox foreigners and painted them as no more than misguided scoundrels who were just a little rough around the edges. Their conversion, said the pope, was "not an event, but a process which would inevitably take time to complete." With the wisdom of hindsight, the Rouenians might have been right to harbor doubts about the Vikings after all.

Now that Rollo was in Francia, he expected to reap the rewards he had been promised, but the crumbling churches, tilting houses, and neglected stretches of withered earth around him looked anything but promising. Growing weary of Rouen, he summoned his cortège and expressed to them his sentiments. It was then that one of them pointed out the lush patch of land just a bit to the south of Rouen. This place, known to the locals as "Les Damps," classed as a minor territory belonging to Charles the Bald (and later his successor, Charles the Fat), the Frankish king of West Francia. Said the Viking to Rollo, "[Les Damps] is plentifully furnished. It has an abundant supply of all kinds of fruits. It is shady with trees, divided up by rivers filled with fish, copiously supplied with various kings of wild game. But it has no armed men and warriors. Let us subordinate the land and reign. We will claim this land as our allotment. Through battle, we will get villages and fortresses, and large and small towns of neighboring peoples, so that the throngs we have left behind far away from here, may rest."

His subordinate's spirited response was enough to spur Rollo into action. He marshaled his crew at once, which had swelled to almost twice its size since his escapades in the Netherlands, and sailed to Les Damps. Just as the Viking predicted, there were almost no royal soldiers posted in the territory, allowing them to seize the unguarded municipality, loot it, and destroy it with ease. Survivors staggered towards the court palace of the West Frankish kingdom and alerted the officials about the swarm of Vikings at the "crossroads of Francia." Though these Viking attacks were nothing new, Frankish authorities, still bickering amongst themselves, were caught off guard by Rollo's unannounced appearance. Recalling the bloodbath that resulted from the Viking massacre of Nantes just a few decades ago, they mobilized their troops and sent them off to the Eure river bank by the commune of Pont-de-l'Arche, on the northwestern neck of Les Damps. There, they engaged in a brief scuffle with the Vikings, but they promptly drew back when they realized that they were in over their heads. Among those who first called for the retreat was a general by the name of Ragnold, a count from West Francia. The thought of it repulsed him, but at this rate, the Norman Franks had already exhausted most, if not all of their options, and the teetering kingdom could not afford any more false moves. Thus, Ragnold bit his tongue and enlisted the aid of one of their former foes – a ruthless warrior by the name of Anstign.

Anstign soared to kingdom-wide infamy as a merciless invader of Francia and Italy, but it was his ingenious snare and assault tactics that made even the most hardened generals shiver. One such tactic is exhibited in the ambush he lay upon a town in West Francia prior to his treaty with the Frankish king in 875. His instructions for the ambush sounded simple enough: "When night is falling, notify the prelate and the count that I am dead. Earnestly request, weeping greatly, that they have me buried, a neophyte, in their town...Make a bier for me, and place me on it as if I were dead. Place my arms in it with me, and lament well as you station yourselves in a ring around them."

Anstign's men carried out his orders to the letter. They were, in fact, such credible thespians that the fateful funeral in the church monastery was attended by almost all in the city; many even brought flowers, emblems, and small presents with them. As planned, the unsuspecting grievers encircled the bier, and as they began to sing their mournful odes, Anstign unsheathed his sword and plunged it into the prelate hovering above him. The attendees dispersed before the Bible in the prelate's hand even hit the ground, but it was too late, as they were surrounded. Anstign's men bolted the doors shut and smote each and every one of them, as Dudo put it, like "wolves do within pens of sheep."

Anstign showed some reluctance when Ragnold's delegates approached him, but they eventually succeeded in persuading him to meet with the Vikings. The next morning, Anstign set off to meet the Vikings, taking with him a pair of warriors fluent in the Dacian language. Locating Rollo in the camp they had pitched by the riverbank, the gruff Anstign skipped the pleasantries and demanded that the Viking chief confess his intentions. To this, Rollo reportedly responded, "We have come from Dacia to take Francia by assault." Anstign was spooked by not only the magnitude of the destruction he was bearing witness to for the first time, but the ice-cold indifference in Rollo's words. When the Vikings made it known that they would never bow down before Charles the Bald, he collected the delegates and scurried back to Ragnold as quickly as his legs could carry him.

He relayed the bad news to the count. "That nation is so strong in youthful age," Anstign warned him. "So well-versed in arms, and tested in many battles. If it is attacked, great peril will be created for us."

Ragnold was outraged. His spirits were already dampened by the absence of Anstign's warriors, but the last thing he had expected was for their last resort to bail on him altogether. Sensing Ragnold's despair, a flag-bearer named Rotland chimed into the conversation. "Why are you all looking to Anstign?" Rotland scoffed. "A wolf will never be captured by a wolf, nor a fox by a fox."

The Franks – particularly Ragnold and Rotland – would have done well to take heed of Anstign's advice. After all, who better to dissect the mind of a marauder than another marauder himself? In any case, Ragnold began to make preparations for an attack on the Vikings, eventually roping Anstign into the deal.

However, before Ragnold and Anstign could even settle upon the details of the attack in question, the Vikings, once again leaps and bounds ahead of their foes, had already constructed a fortress of their own. The makeshift fortress, which consisted of a ring-shaped bulwark built out of "rent earth" and a lofty clay mound that functioned as defensive tower, was plain and unspectacular compared to that of the Frankish kings, but it was sturdy, and it did the job.

The Frankish forces arrived a few days later, with the overeager Rotland spearheading the pack. Disregarding the cautions of Anstign, Rotland and his men charged through the uncannily wide gate of the clay castle and were immediately struck down by the Vikings. Startled by the number of mangled bodies that littered the Vikings' fortress, Ragnold, Anstign, and the remaining Frankish soldiers darted off in the opposite direction.

Yet again, the constricting hands of confusion kneaded his brain as he watched the Frankish soldiers gallop off into the distance. "What evil have we done to the Franks?" Rollo wondered aloud. "Why did they leap on us?...They initiated this evil. The fault is the attacker's, not the defender's. The audacity is his who wishes to strike, not his who defends himself. From now on, whatever evil we might do to them, will be done because their own deeds were a cause of offense... In return for their offenses, let us return like for like, now that such great evils have accumulated...Let us occupy their fortresses and towns!"

The Vikings vacated their rent-earth fortress and moved on to Meulan. Once they had ransacked the town, they killed its inhabitants and picked off its leaders, leaving few survivors in their rage. They then turned their attention to Ragnold and his men, who were recuperating in the woods on the fringes of Meulan. The count attempted to stun the Vikings with a force twice as large as the one that descended upon the fortress, but even then, they were trounced by Rollo and his men. When Ragnold finally resigned to their certain defeat, he made a bid for his freedom, only to be fatally skewered by a Viking spear before he could complete his escape.

Rollo's relentless rampage against the Franks did not stop there. After slaughtering and enslaving another round of soldiers and civilians, Rollo ordered his men back into the ship and directed them to Paris, where they would soon take part in one of the most catastrophic Viking raids the city had ever seen.

Acquiring Normandy

"There seldom is a single wave." – An ancient proverb from the Viking Age

Two years after the Sack of Nantes, another throng of Vikings rowed up the Seine and incited pandemonium in Paris. Taking advantage of the former duchy's lax security, three separate hordes revisited the chaos in the early 860s, and they fled with all the treasure they could carry home.

In an effort to end their quandary once and for all, two bridges were built under the orders of the Edict of Pistres, which flanked the Ile dela Cité and stretched over the Seine at Paris and Pîtres. Due to the speed of the construction, these austere eyesores were nothing to write home about, but these very bridges would play an instrumental role in the Parisians' defense for the upcoming siege.

Robert the Strong, appointed by Charles the Bald as the *major palatii* of West Francia, was entrusted with the governance of the lands between the Seine and Loire Valley, Paris included. Not one to slack on his responsibilities, Robert began the renovations of the Parisian fortress, all the while doing his best to keep the recurring raiders at bay. When Robert was killed during a collision with Vikings at Brissarthe, his son Odo (also known as Eudes) was awarded the title.

Matters continued to dim as authorities in West Francia – which was already embroiled in a centuries-old power struggle thanks to the simultaneous rulers of the Carolingian empire – turned on one another. The western half of the Frankish kingdom experienced an abnormally high turnover rate of kings until Charles the Fat, King of Germany and Italy, came into the picture. The coronation of the plump king led some to anticipate the long-awaited reunification of the faltering Carolingian empire, but this sparkle of hope was quickly snatched away from them. Regardless, Odo was determined to hold down the fort, literally.

Sigfred, the grand patriarch of the Danish Vikings, made a bold demand for payment from the kingdom of West Francia in early 885, only to be snubbed by both Charles and Odo. Wildly offended by the seemingly deteriorating kingdom's rejection, the vengeful Viking mustered an astounding fleet of 700 ships and filled them with some 30,000-40,000 of the finest Vikings near and far, Rollo and his cut-throat warriors included. With the Vikings fast approaching, Odo hastened to the "bridgeheads" by the Seine, strengthening and making last-minute additions to the two towers he had established there. Though he had several royal and aristocratic troops on his side of the court, such as that of the abbot of Saint-Germain-des-Prés and his brother, Robert, he had no more than 200 armed men to spare for the towers at the bridges. This is precisely what made the ensuing events so stupefying to the Vikings, and even the Franks themselves.

Upon the Vikings' arrival on the 25th of November that year, Sigfred granted the Parisians one last chance, ordering them to relinquish to him all of the duchy's treasures at once, but again, the locals refused them. To discipline them for their insubordination, the Vikings launched an attack on the northeast tower at the crack of dawn the next morning, pelting the towers with arrows, boulders, and debris via catapults and mangonels. What the Vikings assumed would be another straightforward victory, however, was anything but. As the Vikings attempted to slam their way into the tower gates, casks of scalding-hot wax and tar rained down on them. The Vikings sustained such severe wounds that they had no choice but to retreat, allowing the Parisians to add an extra story to their towers overnight.

On the 27th of November, a new batch of Vikings returned to the tower – this time, carting with them double the catapults, rams, "mining tools," and flaming projectiles. To their increasing consternation, they were once again thwarted. Even more distressing, none of the sieges they endeavored for the next few months – which included failed attempts at seizing the main water source and blazing decoy longships that fizzled out before they even reached the bridges – produced any momentum. On the 3rd of February, the demoralized and disillusioned soldiers abandoned the towers, supposedly so disheartened that they left their rams by the bridges.

The siege dragged on for about another month, and though the Vikings achieved small victories in Chartres, Le Mans, and Evreux, they were hanging on by the flimsiest of threads. The Parisian defenders were equally beat. At long last, in March of 886, Odo, accompanied by Abbot Joselin of St. Germain, approached Siegfred and offered him approximately 60 pounds of silver to withdraw his forces and commit to a mutual ceasefire. Siegfred accepted the silver at once, and true to his word, he began to gather his men, directing them to Bayeux. The compliant Vikings, who were itching for a change of scenery, followed suit, but Rollo, along with a handful of his bull-headed peers, were not at all satisfied with the measly 60 pounds of silver and insisted upon continuing the fight. As such, Rollo and his loyal followers stayed put, prolonging what appeared to be a fruitless and pitiful siege.

Setting out to prove his naysayers wrong, Rollo and his men put up a valiant effort, even succeeding in assassinating Count Henry of Saxony, but their attempt at besieging Paris later that summer again met with failure. It was only after the arrival of the Imperial Army in October that Rollo and his men agreed to lift the siege. Rather than snuff out what was left of this band of Vikings, King Charles capitalized on the fierce mercenaries at his disposal and tasked them with flattening the revolt in Burgundy in exchange for 700 livres, a bill that was footed in full when they returned the following year.

Rollo, who saw the appeal of a somewhat stable income, hoped to receive another assignment from the Frankish king, only to hear the news of Charles being abruptly dethroned in 888. Thrust into the abyss of aimlessness once more, Rollo and his men roamed up and down Francia, looking for towns to plunder, but over time, such a lifestyle proved unsustainable for the aging Rollo and his breathless men. This became starkly clear when their resources and supplies began to run low around 891. Hoping to conclude their nomadic adventures with one last hurrah, Rollo and his men made their way to Bayeux, the same town looted by Siegfred just 5 years ago. The moment they alighted their longships, the Vikings drew their swords and clashed with the locals' defensive troops. Instead of cowering before them as they did with the last wave of Vikings, the citizens, who had been given plenty of time to bolster their defenses, countered their attack with great vigor. Not only did they resist, they snared Botho, a Norman count in Rollo's crew. The flustered Vikings pressed the authorities of Bayeux for Botho's release and promised them a year's worth of their services and their guardianship in return. Intrigued, the authorities convened to weigh Rollo's proposal, with the pros ultimately tipping the scales. Some worried about the sincerity of the Vikings, but more were anxious about the escalation of the tension between them, which could evolve into a full-fledged war with the intruders. Frankly, a mere count was simply not worth the risk.

Following Botho's release, the Vikings flitted from one Francian village to another, but as soon as the pact began to inch closer towards its expiration date, Rollo and his men filed into their ships and sailed towards Bayeux. Exactly 365 days later, the rejuvenated Vikings barged into the city and pillaged it.

This time around, Rollo included in his spoils a special present for himself. This present was none other than an intoxicating 19-year-old maiden named Poppa. Like many of the aforementioned figures, historians have yet to agree upon Poppa's identity. Some chroniclers credit her as the daughter of Berenger II of Neustria, whereas others believe her the offspring of Count Pepin de Pronne of Vermandois and Lord of Saint Quentin, who himself was the son of the Italian King Bernard and the grandson of Charlemagne. It is unclear whether the relationship between Rollo and Poppa was bound by *more danico* (a type of Nordic open marriage from the olden days), or if it was a purely carnal affair. Whatever the case, they produced William Longsword, Rollo's designated heir. According to William of Jumieges, Poppa bore for Rollo another two daughters, Guillame and Gerloc, with the latter marrying William II, Duke of Aquitaine. Aside from that, little is known about them.

Michael Shae's picture of a statue of William Longsword in Falaise

What transpired in Rollo's life between the birth of William and the beginning of the 10th century is yet another subject of speculation. Most align themselves with Dudo's account, which places Rollo back in Angles just a few months after his domination of Bayeux. There, he reunited with his old friend, Alstem, and assisted him in suppressing the revolt against his kingdom. He then remained in Angles until the early 900s, enjoying the sweet fruits of his labor, but unable to sever his connection with Francia, he sailed away from Angles and headed for the land of the Franks in 911.

The ever-fickle and self-sabotaging kingdom of West Francia was now governed by one the locals referred to as "King Charles the Simple." As appreciative as he was about the crown to his name, he was fully aware of his subjects' capricious nature, and he constantly fretted about losing the throne. He was far from the kingdom's first choice – in fact, he was the 5th.

When Charles's father, Louis the Stammerer, passed, the kingdom was split between Carloman II and Louis III, birthed by the first and second wives of the deceased king, respectively. The pair ruled jointly until the untimely death of Louis III three years later, rendering Carloman the sole ruler of Francia. Another two years later, Carloman, who followed his brother to the other side, was replaced by his cousin, Charles the Fat, and later, Odo, in 888. Only after the citizens began to tire of Odo a decade later was Charles the Simple considered, for the citizens demanded a king with "royal Carolingian blood."

As such, Charles saw Rollo's arrival in 911 as a blessing in disguise. On top of the problematic politics, the kingdom was broke, leaving it powerless to maintain its armies and its wobbling infrastructure in desperate need of repairs. Furthermore, food production in the lands around the Seine, mainly due to the incessant Viking attacks, was at an all-time low. The kingdom's depleted treasury meant that they were unable to fork over the gold, silver, and jewelry that the Vikings were hungry for. Having said that, not all hope was lost, for Charles had in mind an offer he was certain the Vikings could not refuse: precious land.

Regrettably, Charles was shot down by the nobility. As a result, Rollo and his men ran unchecked through the Parisian streets, reducing village after village to ashes before eventually making their way to the affluent and holy city of Chartres. Fortunately for the Franks, those at Chartres triumphantly repelled the Vikings, driving them off to Rouen.

Despite the defeat of the Vikings, Charles knew it would only be a matter of time before they struck again. In a bid to pacify this unremitting headache for good, he overrode the opposition from the nobility and sent the Bishop of Rouen to the Vikings to give them his original offer.

The agreement was finalized in the neutral territory of St. Clair by the River Epte on the 1st of September, 911. Charles bestowed upon Rollo the fertile farmlands bordering the English Channel, including Rouen, to the mouth of the River Seine, a region to be known as the "Duchy of Normandy." In exchange for these lavish terrains, stipulated the Treaty of St. Clair-sur-Epte, Rollo was to pledge an oath of imperishable fidelity and allegiance to the Frankish king.

Rumor has it that the Frankish officials urged Rollo to kneel before Charles and plant a kiss upon his feet as a customary display of deferential respect to the king, but Rollo, who vowed to bow to no one but God, signaled for the most powerfully-built *thegn* to tackle the task instead. In classic Viking fashion, the devious *thegn* bent over, seized Charles by the ankle, and straightened himself up again, sending the king crashing to the ground before kissing his royal feet.

Apart from the pledge of feudal allegiance, the treaty also called for the baptism of Rollo, as well as the marital union of the Viking chieftain and Charles's illegitimate daughter, Gisela of

Francia. The pair had two daughters, Kadline and Niederga. Sadly, this marriage was short-lived, for Gisela demanded a divorce from the mentally and physically abusive Rollo not long after the birth of their second daughter. Some say he rekindled his romance with Poppa a few years later.

Little information about Rollo's rule as the Duke of Normandy survives, but the following passage from *The Vikings*, authored by Robert Wernick, sheds a bit of light upon the chieftain's reign, one as brutal as it was progressive: "[W]hen some peasants sought the right to hunt and fish in Rollo's woods, lakes, and rivers, he dispatched his uncle, Count Rudolph, to cut off a hand and a foot of each of the would-be-poachers. But he was also sharp-witted and practical. He let himself be baptized, and he lost no time in restoring the churches that he and his fellow Vikings had sacked..." Others recall a white-robed Rollo lumbering up and down the streets of Rouen, dishing out food, clothes, and alms to the poor.

The latter years of Rollo's life may be cloaked in uncertainty, but his prestigious legacy still shines through in the diverse, bustling, and vibrant region that is Normandy today. He will forever be remembered by the locals as the progenitor of a powerful bloodline – from William Longsword to William the Conqueror, 11th century Duke of Normandy and the King of England. His family tree also included Lord Roger II, founder of the Kingdom of Sicily, which transformed Normandy into a "bourgeois powerhouse."

Rollo retired in 927 and died around three years later, with his body buried in the Cathedral of Rouen. Though he was never granted the eternal life promised to him by the prophecy, he laid himself to rest knowing that he had found his home.

Frederic Bisson's picture of a statue of Rollo in Rouen

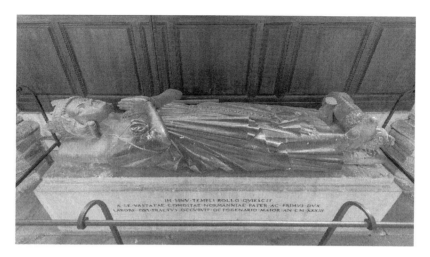

Raimond Spekking's picture of Rollo's grave in the Cathedral of Rouen

Online Resources

Other books about Viking history by Charles River Editors

Other books about Rollo on Amazon

Further Reading

Lansing, M. F. (2016). ROLLO THE VIKING. Retrieved February 27, 2018, from http://www.mainlesson.com/display.php?author=lansing&book=barbarian&story=rollo

Sutherland, A. (2017, October 5). Rollo: Viking Sea Lord, Chieftain And The First Ruler Of Normandy. Retrieved February 28, 2018, from http://www.ancientpages.com/2017/10/05/rollo-Viking-sea-lord-chieftain-first-ruler-normandy/

Editors, A. P. (2017, January 22). Mystery Of Viking Ruler Rollo Continues – Surprising Discovery In Ancient Grave. Retrieved February 28, 2018, from http://www.ancientpages.com/2017/01/22/mystery-of-Viking-ruler-rollo-continues-surprising-discovery-in-ancient-grave/

Kinnes, T. (2016). Rollo and the Relatives - Section 11. Retrieved February 28, 2018, from http://oaks.nvg.org/rollo.html

Editors, S. N. (2013, October 20). Who Was Gange Rolf? Retrieved February 28, 2018, from http://sonsofnorwayblog.blogspot.tw/2013/10/who-was-gange-rolf.html

Kinnes, T. (2015). Tales from Dudo's Norman History. Retrieved February 28, 2018, from http://oaks.nvg.org/dudo3.html

Hurst, D. (2009). Rollo Rognvaldsson "The Dane" Duke of Normandy. Retrieved February 28, 2018, from http://www.deloriahurst.com/deloriahurst%20page/3310.html

Douglasson, H. (2008, March 31). A Viking childhood. Retrieved February 28, 2018, from http://www.bbc.co.uk/northyorkshire/content/articles/2005/10/05/Viking_childhood_feature.shtml

Editors, A. P. (2016, November 1). What Was Life For Ancient Viking Children? Retrieved February 28, 2018, from http://www.ancientpages.com/2016/11/01/life-ancient-Viking-children/

Ladegaard, I. (2012, November 19). How Vikings killed time. Retrieved February 28, 2018, from http://sciencenordic.com/how-Vikings-killed-time

Editors, B. A. (2013, September 23). The Story of Rollo the Viking............the rest is HISTORY. Retrieved February 28, 2018, from https://boothancestry.wordpress.com/2013/09/23/the-story-of-rollo-the-Viking-the-rest-is-history/

Dzhak, Y. (2016, May 13). The Viking Sieges of Paris. Retrieved February 28, 2018, from https://www.warhistoryonline.com/medieval/Vikings-sieges-paris.html

Editors, E. H. (2017, February 7). Rollo and the Foundation of Normandy. Retrieved February 28, 2018, from https://exploringhist.blogspot.tw/2017/02/rollo-and-foundation-of-normandy.html

Editors, N. D. (2017, August 9). HISTORICAL TRUTH OF ROLLO. Retrieved February 28, 2018, from https://inventorybag.com/blogs/normandescendants/historical-truth-of-rollo

Haaren, J. H. (2004, August). Rollo the Viking. Retrieved February 28, 2018, from http://www.authorama.com/famous-men-of-the-middle-ages-15.html

Editors, H. K. (2012). Rollo The Viking. Retrieved February 28, 2018, from http://www.historyforkids.net/rollo-the-Viking.html

Editors, H. C. (2017). HOW A VIKING LAID THE GROUNDWORK FOR THE KING OF ENGLAND. Retrieved February 28, 2018, from http://www.history.co.uk/shows/the-real-Vikings/articles/how-a-Viking-laid-the-groundwork-for-the-king-of-england

Editors, F. H. (2014, March 14). Rollo, Viking Count of Normandy. Retrieved February 28, 2018, from https://thefreelancehistorywriter.com/2014/03/14/rollo-Viking-count-of-normandy/

McKay, B., & McKay, K. (2016, January 31). The 80 Wisdom Sayings of the Vikings. Retrieved February 29, 2018, from https://www.artofmanliness.com/2016/01/31/the-80-wisdom-sayings-of-the-Vikings/

Butler, C. (2007). FC40: The rise of the Franks (c.500-841). Retrieved February 29, 2018, from http://www.flowofhistory.com/units/birth/5/FC40

Nelson, L. H. (2014). The Rise of the Franks, 330-751. Retrieved February 29, 2018, from http://www.vlib.us/medieval/lectures/franks_rise.html

Mayer, E. (2012, December 29). The Rise of the Franks. Retrieved February 29, 2018, from http://www.emayzine.com/index.php/history-103/history-103-week-3/122-the-rise-of-the-franks

Harding, S. B. (2015). RISE OF THE FRANKS. Retrieved February 29, 2018, from http://www.mainlesson.com/display.php?author=harding&book=middle&story=franks

Editors, H. W. (2016). HISTORY OF THE FRANKS . Retrieved February 29, 2018, from http://www.historyworld.net/wrldhis/PlainTextHistories.asp?historyid=ab74

Editors, L. (2016, March 30). 10 MAJOR ACCOMPLISHMENTS OF CHARLEMAGNE. Retrieved February 29, 2018, from https://learnodo-newtonic.com/charlemagne-accomplishments

Budde, P. (2017). Lotharingia, East and West Francia – 843-1100. Retrieved February 29, 2018, from http://paulbuddehistory.com/europe/the-emergence-of-lotharingia/

Adrien, C. J. (2016, October 22). The City the Vikings Sacked Before Paris, and Why It Matters. Retrieved February 29, 2018, from https://cjadrien.com/Viking-sack-nantes/

Editors, W. P. (2014, March 12). The Viking Sack of Nantes. Retrieved February 29, 2018, from https://thewildpeak.wordpress.com/2014/03/12/the-Viking-sack-of-nantes/

Editors, B. (2014, April 1). Charles III Biography. Retrieved February 29, 2018, from https://www.biography.com/people/charles-iii-37946

Kinnes, T. (2011). HARALD HARFAGER'S SAGA. Retrieved February 29, 2018, from http://oaks.nvg.org/hk3.html

Editors, T. H. (2013). About the hoard. Retrieved February 29, 2018, from http://www.teachinghistory100.org/objects/about_the_object/Viking_treasure

Editors, M. (2018, January 13). Rollo the Viking Duke of Normandy. Retrieved February 29, 2018, from http://mythologian.net/rollo-Viking-duke-normandy/

Quill, S. (2014, August 20). Viking childhood. Retrieved February 29, 2018, from https://sandyquill.com/tag/Viking-childhood/

Short, W. R. (2012). Viking Ships. Retrieved February 29, 2018, from http://www.hurstwic.org/history/articles/manufacturing/text/norse_ships.htm

Lau, J. (2017). Rollo (846-930 AD). Retrieved February 29, 2018, from http://www.storiespreschool.com/rollo.html

Editors, D. Y. (2016, June 23). 10 Viking Proverbs You Should Know. Retrieved February 29, 2018, from http://thedockyards.com/10-Viking-proverbs-know/

Editors, T. F. (2017, December 11). Feux de la Saint Jean - Summer Solstice. Retrieved March 1, 2018, from https://www.travelfranceonline.com/feux-de-la-saint-jean-summer-solstice/

Price, N. S. (2015). THE VIKINGS IN BRITTANY. Retrieved March 1, 2018, from http://vsnrweb-publications.org.uk/The%20Vikings%20In%20Brittany.pdf

Editors, D. N. (2015, April 22). Viking Clothing - What did the Vikings Wear? Retrieved March 1, 2018, from https://www.danishnet.com/Vikings/Viking-clothing-what-did-Vikings-wear/

Editors, G. (2017, October 12). Rollo Ragnvaldsson. Retrieved March 1, 2018, from https://www.geni.com/people/Gange-Hr%C3%B3lfr-Rollo-of-Normandy/2915061

MacIsaac, T. (2014, December 16). A Step Closer to the Mysterious Origin of the Viking Sword Ulfberht. Retrieved March 1, 2018, from http://www.ancient-origins.net/artifacts-ancient-technology/step-closer-mysterious-origin-Viking-sword-ulfberht-002455

Short, W. R. (2017). Knattleikr, the Viking Ball Game. Retrieved March 1, 2018, from http://www.hurstwic.org/history/articles/daily_living/text/knattleikr.htm

Editors, E. B. (2012, February 6). Harald I. Retrieved March 1, 2018, from https://www.britannica.com/biography/Harald-I-king-of-Norway

Bryant, W. (2017, February 27). What were Viking generals/leaders/captains called? Retrieved March 1, 2018, from https://www.quora.com/What-were-Viking-generals-leaders-captains-called

Editors, N. T. (2016, October 16). What The Vikings REALLY Drank... Retrieved March 1, 2018, from https://www.norsetradesman.com/blogs/news/what-did-Vikings-drink

Editors, F. V. (2013, November 7). The Angles (Ingles, English – Danish Expansion and Anglish Migration). Retrieved March 1, 2018, from http://freya.theladyofthelabyrinth.com/?page_id=618

Editors, C. C. (2017). Rollo Rognvaldsson. Retrieved March 1, 2018, from http://www.inthechickencoop.us/notables/rollo/

Milsom, M. (2014). Dudo of St. Quentin's Gesta Normannorum. Retrieved March 1, 2018, from http://www.michael-milsom.org.uk/mdm/rollo/rollo11.htm

Green, R. W. (2016). Harald Hildetand . Retrieved March 1, 2018, from http://willofjehovah.com/Family%20History/_Rowe/from%20Adam/__harald%20hildetand/___1st%20Edition/__harald%20hildetand.htm

Editors, E. N. (2017). Rollo and the Norman colony. Retrieved March 1, 2018, from https://erenow.com/postclassical/theVikingsahistory/10.html

Editors, A. (2015). Chapter 8. Retrieved March 1, 2018, from https://www.arlima.net/the-orb/orb_done/dudo/08-franci

Assaf, B. R. (2017, December 26). Radbod, King of the Frisians. Retrieved March 1, 2018, from https://www.geni.com/people/Radbod-King-of-the-Frisians/6000000003828105626

Ager, B. (2011, March 29). Viking Weapons and Warfare. Retrieved March 1, 2018, from http://www.bbc.co.uk/history/ancient/Vikings/weapons_01.shtml#five

McCoy, D. (2015). VIKING RAIDS AND WARFARE. Retrieved March 1, 2018, from https://norse-mythology.org/Viking-raids-warfare/

Kane, N. (2016, June 23). Viking Battle Tactics: The Boar Formation. Retrieved March 1, 2018, from http://spangenhelm.com/Viking-battle-tactics-boar-formation/

Editors, V. T. (2013, October). 843 - Vikings attacked Nantes. Retrieved March 1, 2018, from https://Vikinghistorytales.blogspot.tw/2013/10/843-Vikings-attacked-nantes.html

Milsom, M. (2014). Dudo of St. Quentin's Gesta Normannorum. Retrieved March 2, 2018, from http://www.michael-milsom.org.uk/mdm/rollo/rollo10.htm

Lifshitz, F. (2013). Dudo of St. Quentin's Gesta Normannorum. Retrieved March 2, 2018, from https://www.arlima.net/the-orb/orb_done/dudo/dudindexe.html

Kinnes, T. (2015). Part 2. The work of Dudo and what it is about. Retrieved March 2, 2018, from http://oaks.nvg.org/dudo2.html

Sewell, R. (2011). The Ancestry of Poppa: Wife of Rolf the Ganger. Retrieved March 2, 2018, from http://www.robertsewell.ca/poppa.html

Editors, W. A. (2014, July 9). Viking Origins: Rollo Ragnsvaldsson. Retrieved March 2, 2018, from http://walkingwithancestors.blogspot.tw/2014/07/my-Viking-origins-rollo-ragnsvaldsson.html

Editors, N. D. (2016). Charles the Bald. Retrieved March 2, 2018, from http://www.nndb.com/people/183/000093901/

Snell, M. (2017, December 3). Charles III Biography. Retrieved March 2, 2018, from https://www.thoughtco.com/charles-ii-profile-1788673

Editors, V. R. (2012, December). My Favorite Norse Proverbs and Sayings. Retrieved March 2, 2018, from http://www.Vikingrune.com/2012/12/norse-proverbs-and-sayings/

Editors, E. A. (2010). Siege of Paris (885-886). Retrieved March 2, 2018, from http://enacademic.com/dic.nsf/enwiki/1699607

Editors, F. H. (2015, April 17). The Siege of Paris of 885-886. Retrieved March 2, 2018, from https://thefreelancehistorywriter.com/2015/04/17/the-siege-of-paris-of-885-886/

Editors, B. P. (2014, November 25). Vikings Begin Siege of Paris: Besiegers Driven Off the Following Year. Retrieved March 2, 2018, from http://www.burnpit.us/2014/11/Vikings-begin-siege-paris-besiegers-driven-following-year

Editors, T. H. (2016, September 1). Https://todayinhistory.blog/tag/charles-the-simple/. Retrieved March 2, 2018, from https://todayinhistory.blog/tag/charles-the-simple/

Editors, V. A. (2017, January 31). Charles III the Simple. Retrieved March 2, 2018, from https://www.theVikingarchive.com/charles-iii-the-simple/

Pierre, M. (2014, February 6). Normandy 911. Retrieved March 2, 2018, from http://www.medievalhistories.com/normandy-911/

Riddle, J. M. (2016). *A History of the Middle Ages, 300–1500*. Rowman & Littlefield. Retrieved March 2, 2018.

Sprague, M. (2007). *Norse Warfare: The Unconventional Battle Strategies of the Ancient Vikings*. Hippocrene Books.

Gillingham, J. (2004). *Anglo-Norman Studies XXVI: Proceedings of the Battle Conference 2003*. Boydell Press.

Albu, E. (2001). *The Normans in Their Histories: Propaganda, Myth and Subversion*. Boydell & Brewer.

Abels, R. (2009). *"Alfred the Great and Æthelred II 'the Unready": The Viking Wars in England*. United Naval Academy Press

Free Books by Charles River Editors

We have brand new titles available for free most days of the week. To see which of our titles are currently free, click on this link.

Discounted Books by Charles River Editors

We have titles at a discount price of just 99 cents everyday. To see which of our titles are currently 99 cents, click on this link.

Made in the USA
Monee, IL
28 June 2023

37819682R00022